Storm It!

The Little Book For Brainstorming

Created & Designed By
TeeCee Design Studio

Thank you so much for your purchase.

I really do hope that this book has helped you,
even in some small way.

Would you like to see different designs/styles?

I am always very happy to hear from customers,
so please feel free to email me on

teeceedesignstudio@yahoo.com